Animals Close Up

TURTLES CLOSE UP

By Seth Lynch

Please visit our website, www.garethstevens.com. For a free color catalog of all our high-quality books, call toll free 1-800-542-2595 or fax 1-877-542-2596.

Library of Congress Cataloging-in-Publication Data
Names: Lynch, Seth, author.
Title: Turtles close up / Seth Lynch.
Description: New York : Gareth Stevens Publishing, [2023] | Series: Animals close up | Includes index.
Identifiers: LCCN 2021040551 (print) | LCCN 2021040552 (ebook) | ISBN 9781538281369 (set) | ISBN 9781538281376 (library binding) | ISBN 9781538281352 (paperback) | ISBN 9781538281383 (ebook)
Subjects: LCSH: Turtles–Juvenile literature.
Classification: LCC QL666.C5 L96 2023 (print) | LCC QL666.C5 (ebook) | DDC 597.92–dc23
LC record available at https://lccn.loc.gov/2021040551
LC ebook record available at https://lccn.loc.gov/2021040552

First Edition

Published in 2023 by
Gareth Stevens Publishing
29 East 21st Street
New York, NY 10010

Copyright © 2023 Gareth Stevens Publishing

Editor: Kristen Nelson
Designer: Rachel Rising

Photo credits: Cover, p. 1 Fajar Tri Amboro/Shutterstock.com; p. 5 Geofox/Shutterstock.com; p. 7 Agami Photo Agency/Shutterstock.com; p. 9 Marc Parsons/Shuttestock.com; p. 11 Gerry Bishop/Shutterstock.com; p. 13 Minnows432/Shutterstock.com; p. 15 xbrchx/Shutterstock.com; pp. 17, 24 blue-sea.cz/Shutterstock.com; p. 19 danz13/Shutterstock.com; p. 21 fztommy/Shutterstock.com; pp. 23, 24 Rich Carey/Shutterstock.com.

All rights reserved. No part of this book may be reproduced in any form without permission in writing from the publisher, except by a reviewer.

Printed in the United States of America

CPSIA compliance information: Batch #CSGS23: For further information contact Gareth Stevens, New York, New York at 1-800-542-2595.

Contents

So Many Turtles 4

That Turtle Look 8

Super Shell 16

Water Time 18

Words to Know 24

Index. 24

Turtles live all over
the world.
There are more than
300 kinds!

They may be big or small. Leatherbacks are the biggest!

Turtles have two eyes.
They do not have ears.

They do not have teeth.

They may be brown or black.
They may be green.

Some have stripes.
These may be yellow,
orange, or red.

They have a bony shell.
It has two parts.

Most turtles
can hide in it!

They have webbed toes.
These help with swimming.

Sea turtles
have flippers!

Words to Know

flipper   shell

Index

colors 12, 14   size 6

flippers 22   shell 6